THE GREATER
POSSIBILITIES

Thom Rutledge

THE GREATER
POSSIBILITIES

*125 Reflections on the
Method & Meaning of
Genuine Success*

THOM RUTLEDGE
Author of *Embracing Fear*

Thom Rutledge

Copyright 2016 Thom Rutledge

Thom Rutledge

331 22nd Ave North, Suite One

Nashville, TN 37203

(615) 327-3423

thomrutledgeauthor@gmail.com

www.thomrutledge.com

Join Thom on Facebook:

www.facebook.com/thom.rutledge.9

ISBN-13 978-1523392124

Thom Rutledge

For Joyce Marie Choate

An undiscovered talent

1930 - 2002

————————

At first something seems impossible, then it becomes improbable but with enough conviction and support, it finally becomes inevitable.   –Christopher Reeve

We cannot solve problems by using the same kind of thinking we used when we created them. –Albert Einstein

You can't have what you want unless you dare to see things through. –Jerry Jeff Walker

Thom Rutledge

CONTENTS

Thom Rutledge

Preface

Just as I was putting the finishing touches on my first book (Simple Truth), way back in the 1900's, I walked into the self-help section of one of my favorite bookstores. (Remember bookstores?). I stood there looking up and down and all around at the gazillion self-help books there and felt all the excitement of publishing my first book drain out of me. Who was I to think I had anything to contribute to those self-help stacks?

Spending time later that day with my friend and mentor, Lily Whitehawk, I described my experience in the bookstore to her. "I don't have anything to say that has not already been said," I said.

"Of course you don't," Lily said.

What?! Crap. This woman for whom I have great respect, this woman I trust completely, was agreeing with me, confirming the conclusion I had reached in the bookstore. What little was left of my self-confidence slipped away.

Then Lily continued, "but there are people out there waiting for the way you are going to say it."

Oh.

Welcome to *The Greater Possibilities*, the essence of what I have to say – the way I say it. My wish is that this little book can contribute to what you have to say and how you say it.

Thom Rutledge

Introduction

There are probably as many definitions for success as there are people who want to succeed. And the targets for our efforts are many. We want to succeed in business. We want to be successful husbands and wives and parents. We want to whittle that golf score down to size. We want to be successful students, whether we are nineteen trying to decide on a major, or 45 trying to master that new computer program, or reaching for that promotion.

More of us than ever are aware of the importance of feeling a sense of purpose in the work we do. We want to succeed spiritually --- that is, we want to effectively apply what we believe deep in our hearts to our day-to-day lives. Along with material success, we want to experience the power of genuine fulfillment. The potential for this success belongs to every one of us. The power we seek is not power over other people, or even power over life's circumstances. The power of true success is revealed when we can learn (with lots of practice) to see past the barrage of daily distractions, setting illusion aside in favor of the real magic that emerges from deep within us when we become willing to do whatever it takes to succeed from the inside out. Only then will we discover the greater possibilities.

Whatever your definition for success, wherever your sights are set, here is a little book full of simple, but powerful ideas, suggestions and lessons that will improve your chances of hitting the mark.

Ready, Aim ...

Letting Go

Thom Rutledge

Forget about Control

One of the keys to success is accepting full responsibility for yourself. Accepting this responsibility, contrary to popular belief, has nothing to do with being "in control." There is a major distinction to be made between *being in control* and accepting the responsibility of *being in charge*.

Simply put: You have nothing to say about the cards dealt you, but everything to say about how you will play those cards.

~

Be in charge, but forget about being in control.

Renounce Victimization

Victimization is a state of mind in which you believe that how you are doing in any particular moment is determined more by the circumstances beyond your control than by how you choose to respond to those circumstances.

To accept full responsibility for yourself is to renounce victimization.

Blame & Responsibility

A victim will blame the dealer of the cards, or blame the person who taught him how to play cards, or maybe even the cards themselves. A victim may even take refuge in blaming himself, not understanding that there is an important difference between *assigning blame* and *taking responsibility*.

Reject Self-Blame

To admit that things are not going well in your life because you are a worthless piece of crap is not accepting responsibility. It is quite the opposite. Hiding behind self-blame and drowning in the resulting shame is one of the most efficient --- not to mention prevalent --- ways to avoid personal responsibility.

~

Being a victim is an indulgence
you cannot afford.

Acknowledge the Continuum

None of us are totally immune to victimization. At one time or another, we all think and act as victim, and we all think and act responsibly at other times. It would be a mistake to claim that you are *always* a victim, or that you accept full responsibility for yourself *all of the time.*

Think of responsibility as a continuum along which you will move back and forth, depending on any number of variables.

Constant Motion

To enhance your chances for success, you will do well to perceive yourself in realistic terms along the continuum, and focus your efforts toward accepting full responsibility one day at a time. Remembering that you are in constant motion along the continuum of responsibility is a powerful antidote to that pesky perfectionism.

~

Change is constant. You are always in motion along the continuum.

Be Realistic

To be successful you must become both optimistic *and* realistic. This requires that you come to terms with your own human imperfection. To pretend that your very real human flaws do not exist is certain self-sabotage, as is thinking of yourself as nothing but flaws.

~

*The big let go is made of
lots of little let go's.*

Let Go of Perfection

A perfectionist is not someone who does things perfectly; a perfectionist is someone who believes she is supposed to do things perfectly. Perfectionism is a condition of constant pain and self-absorption.

Contrary to popular opinion, striving for perfection is not productive; it is destructive --- at it's worst, suicidal. By constantly expecting the impossible of yourself (perfection), you set yourself up to fail --- over and over again.

Do Your Best

Do the very best you can. Challenge yourself to stretch beyond your current level of competence, but do not expect the impossible. Do not expect perfection.

~

Perfectionism is a state of constant self-victimization.

Perfectionism's Energy Source

In your efforts (imperfect efforts) to recognize that perfection is not even one of your choices, you will come face to face with perfectionism's energy source: *self-criticism*. You must learn to identify and reject the highly negative-biased view (opinions) associated with your self-critical thinking.

~

Self-condemnation has nothing
to do with being responsible.

Perfectionism's Antidote

When you fall, get up.

When you forget, remember.

Expect to fall and to forget.

~

You will always be

perfectly imperfect.

Too Much Humble Pie

Everyone has known someone who apologizes incessantly. "I'm sorry about this, I'm sorry about that, I'm sorry for everything, even if I had nothing to do with it." These people have eaten one too many slices of humble pie.

And if you confront them with how irritating their constant apologizing is, what do they instantly do? Apologize, of course.

Don't be one of these people, and if you have been, for goodness sake, don't apologize for it.

~

Victimization is a
self-fulfilling prophecy.

Stubborn Answers

Sometimes there are questions that seemingly have no answers. You may spend a great deal of energy trying to find those non-existent answers. Try letting go of the struggle; relax, meditate on something beautiful or pleasurable. These stubborn answers will show up when they are ready ... usually when you least expect it -- and right on time.

~

Let go of your desire for perfection.

Embrace your need for

patience and flexibility.

You're Alive!

When life seems to become one crisis after another, with not much breathing room in between, remember this: All things unfinished or in turmoil around you are reminders that 1.) you are still alive, and 2.) you still have work to do.

Also remember that in spite of what you may believe or what others may tell you, it does not all have to be done today.

A vacation is any moment of

relaxation without guilt.

Imagine that.

Reality

Your competence fluctuates according to countless variables and influences. Progress has many peaks and valleys. Do not insist that your growth be steady and constant. In other words, keep in mind that you are human.

~

Be careful to not make your most recent accomplishment your new minimal expectation.

A Set Up

If you expect to be flawless in your approach toward your goals, you will come face to face with the reality that there is no flawless way to any goal. Instead, expect the flaws to be manageable, and the goals "accomplish-able."

This is how to set yourself up for success.

~

Since you can't fire stress, give it a brief leave of absence now and then.

Try procrastinating stress.

You-nique

There has never been, nor will there ever be, another human being exactly like you. You arrived on this planet with special abilities that are uniquely yours. You also arrived, charged with a mission that only you can accomplish.

~

You can do great things, and

never come close to perfect.

You can fulfill a purpose

and never even know what it was.

Simplicity Works

Medicine does not have to taste bad to be good and the truth you seek is probably not complicated. The greatest truths are simple but it seems inherent to the human condition that we make the work of getting to simplicity such an arduous task.

Let go of your attachment to complexity: let simplicity do its thing.

~

On a bad day, just do your work
and try to be kind.
This is the power of lowered expectations.

Humor

Having a sense of humor is not about being funny. A sense of humor is a sense of perspective, an awareness that every little detail may not be as important as we tend to think.

Learn to laugh, and make sure you practice every day.

~

Practice makes . . . practice.

When in doubt... laugh.

Being Aware

Heart & Mind

The battle between heart and mind is a mistake. Heart and mind are intended as equal partners, not competitors or enemies. The next time you feel the struggle beginning, try letting them sit down together and talk it out.

~

Feelings are not the problem.
They are an important
part of the solution.

The Definition for Sanity

Talking to yourself doesn't mean you are crazy. It means that you are human. We all talk to ourselves and the sooner you acknowledge the many conversations going on within your mind, the better you will be. This is reality; and being in touch with reality is the definition for sanity.

You Are Not Alone

There is a committee that lives and works inside each of us. Familiarize yourself with your committee. Put your ear to the door of the conference room within you. Listen to what is going on in there.

What is your committee talking about?

~

We all talk to ourselves.

We just need to get better at it.

Who is in charge?

Open the door to your inner conference room. Walk in and take a look around, continuing to pay close attention to what is being said, and who is saying it. Does the committee within your mind run smoothly? Does everyone get to have their say? Or is there a bully in charge, monopolizing the goings-on of your committee?

It is not unusual to discover that the "The Big Bully Within" (a powerful, self-critical voice) is standing at the head of the conference table, running the show.

The Bully Within You

Think of yourself as a separate person from your self-critical thinking. Experience yourself not as the one doing the criticizing, but as the one being criticized. Although this is never much fun (standing in the line of self-critical fire), separating from that predictable Bully in your head will create a place for your own opinion, separate from "his."

It takes some time, but with practice you will learn to remain separate from self-critical thought, and ultimately to form your own, more realistic, more positive opinions of yourself.

Disagree with Yourself

Here is some really good news: you don't have to do away with your negative, self-critical thoughts. You don't have to banish them, or conquer them, or plead with them to leave you alone. You just have to learn to disagree with them. Practice disagreeing with your Inner-Bully.

~

To your Inner-Bully, say:

I see you, I hear you, and

I disagree with you.

Civil Disobedience

Even when the most misguided, self-destructive members of your committee seem to be fully in charge --- telling you exactly how to think, what to say, and what to do --- you still have the power of decision on your side. Use that power to disobey those negative forces within you.

~

Even when you tend to agree
with your Inner-Bully,
you can still disobey him.

Beyond Negative

When you put your ear to the conference room door, and you can hear only negative comments and complaints, make a point of continuing to listen. Listen very carefully, listen past the loud negative thoughts, listen for just one hopeful voice.

No matter how small, how distant, or how muffled that hopeful voice may sound, lock onto it. Focus on it. Prepare to rescue it.

The Rescue

When your hopeful voice has been tied up and stuffed into a closet at the back of your conference room, what will you do about it? Close your eyes, take a deep breath and visualize the answer to that question.

Installing a New Leader

You can try firing your Inner-Bully, but usually that doesn't work very well. The better approach is to concentrate on creating a new leader for your committee. The new leader will at first lack credibility, and seemingly lack power, but that is only a matter of persistent practice.

Begin with a commitment to yourself to create a strong, decisive and benevolent new leader for your inner committee. Call your new leader the "Decision Maker."

~

Your new leader, whether
you like it or not... is you.

Don't Do That

Try this: for the next few seconds, do not focus any of your attention on your left hand. Don't think about your left hand, don't let the thought of your left hand even enter your mind.

Now don't think of the color blue, don't think of a purple giraffe, and *don't think negative thoughts!*

The Negative Command

In hypnosis, suggesting that someone *not* focus on that left hand is called a "negative command" and quite simply it demonstrates that our brains cannot encode a negative. In order to even attempt to *not* think of your left hand, your brain must access the idea of your left hand.

Understanding the negative command can save you a lot of time and energy when it comes to replacing the Inner-Bully with your new Decision Maker. Just try *not* listening to your Inner-Bully. See how that goes.

A New Focus

Now that you understand that attempting to not listen to your Inner-Bully is a self-defeating endeavor, you are free to devise a more effective strategy.

Try this: focus your attention on your right foot. Keep your attention on your right foot. When your attention strays from your right foot, gently but firmly bring it back to focusing on your right foot.

The Coup Begins

With this technique (focusing on your right foot), even if your mind tends to drift back to your left hand, you still have a way to succeed --- by focusing your attention specifically elsewhere. The same technique will work as you begin the persistent practice of replacing your Inner-Bully with your Decision Maker as Chairman of the Board.

With the Aid of the Enemy

There is a way for you to actually trick the Inner-Bully into helping you. Instead of hopelessly trying to make self-critical thoughts go away, use them as reminders --- sort of "post-it-notes" of the mind --- to reinforce your newly appointed Decision Maker. Every time you become aware of a destructive, self-critical thought, instantly place a self-supportive, positive thought right next to it. That's all you need to do. Hold your ground.

~

No need to get rid of any thoughts.

Just give yourself a choice.

The Mind's Limitation

Even though your mind is multiple in nature, with many varying thoughts, opinions and feelings existing simultaneously, your mind's conscious focus can only be on one thing at a time. Use this limitation of the mind to your advantage by constantly insisting that your attention be held on the supportive thoughts of your Decision Maker.

~

No two thoughts can occupy the same mind at the same time.

The Greater Possibilities

Any motivational speaker will tell you that in order to succeed, you need to be open to the positive. Learn to see and seek the greater possibilities. Take the time to develop clear images of your goals. Take the risk (and it will feel risky) to practice expecting positive outcomes. When necessary, utilize a simple slogan heard repeatedly in the program of Alcoholics Anonymous: *Fake it 'til you make it.*

~

See clearly. Take action.

Expect results.

Setting Your Sights

Too often you will know much more about what you *don't* want than about what you *do* want. If you stop there, you will not have any idea how to change and you will tend to return to the safe haven of the familiar --- those old patterns of thinking and behaving that you have already proven to be ineffective.

Give yourself the direction you need. Set your sights on specific goals, *your* specific goals.

~

Once you identify something you don't want, put into words, and into a visual image, what you want instead.

Forward Ho!

Look to the past only as long as it takes to learn the lesson. Then, with eyes straight ahead, move forward.

~

Learn from the past
then get the hell out of there.

To Change

If you are constantly trying to change this or that about yourself, if you are endlessly dissatisfied with yourself, try something radical: *self-acceptance.*

~

Each day practice accepting exactly who you are, and you will never stop changing.

The Right Assumptions

Assumptions are natural --- and they can be dangerous. So be sure to make the right assumptions:

• Assume that you will make assumptions.

• Assume that other people don't see the world as you do.

• Assume that others will make assumptions about you.

• Assume that if you want to know what someone else is thinking, you will need to ask.

Your Needs

We are taught to ignore our own needs in our efforts to take care of other people. Being willing to sacrifice and to compromise is an admirable quality, but if you always deny your own needs, you will inevitably become self-absorbed by your own neediness.

~

Self-denial results in dependence.

Self-attention creates independence.

A Trap

Beware of falling into the trap of believing that when you "feel better," you will become motivated to "do better." More times than not, the reverse is true.

~

It is possible to <u>feel</u> very bad,

and still <u>do</u> very good.

Show Respect

One very important way to demonstrate respect is to listen to others with an open mind, and with genuine curiosity. When you do this, you will be showing respect … and you just might learn something.

~

Respect is not necessarily

expressed through agreement.

In Your Opinion

Be careful to distinguish between developing opinions and forming judgments. It is important to have strong beliefs, but if your strong belief becomes inflexible, you will have become a part of the problem.

~

It is useless to be judgmental of judgmental people.

Conversations to Convey

Do you approach conversations like an attorney, always with an agenda, always ready to make your case, always ready to convince the jury? This is not always the best approach, and can lead to a complete break down of communication.

Practice having conversations to *convey* information, rather than to *convince* someone that your position is right. Also listen for what the other person is trying to convey. You might be surprised how often this will solve a problem.

~

Without a shared goal, any attempt

at communication is doomed.

Noisy Guilt

Nowadays highways are constructed with rumble strips between the road and the shoulder of the road. The purpose is to alert us --- wake us up --- when we unknowingly veer of the road. It makes a loud, startling sound to which we automatically respond by straightening our course.

Natural (healthy) guilt works the same way. Once we are back on track --- living within the bounds of our personal value system --- we no longer need the noise.

Neurotic (unhealthy) guilt is the noise at the shoulder of the road that won't stop now matter how straight you drive.

~

The purpose of healthy guilt is to keep you awake, not beat yourself over the head.

Mistakes

Some people are terribly afraid of making mistakes. They may be so afraid that they decide to stop trying to succeed. Here are three important things to know about mistake-making:

1.) Everyone makes mistakes. If someone tells you otherwise, they are mistaken.

2.) Making mistakes does not make you a mistake.

3.) Mistake-making is not only permissible, it is a very important way to learn.

~

Have faith that you will always

make just the right mistake.

A Good Start

When a movie ends with a big wedding, intended to signify the happiest of endings, we know that this is not very realistic. We know that the wedding is not the ending, but the beginning --- hopefully the beginning of lots of joy, but also the beginning of hard work.

Likewise, success is not a happily-ever-after Hollywood ending, but the beginning. Along with the benefits and the celebration, success brings with it responsibility. Treat your success with the spirit of commitment, like a strong, healthy marriage.

~

Question with all your mind.

Believe with all your heart.

Facing Obstacles

Thom Rutledge

Cash Flow

If mental energy was money, how much cash would you be throwing away on self-doubt and self-condemnation every day? Every week? Every year?

~

Are you solving the problems that you want to solve, or the problems that you think you are suppose to solve?

Over-rule the Objection

Sometimes we secretly object to our own success. If deep down you don't feel deserving, you can become your own worst enemy.

When you are not 100% on your own side, be sure to over-rule the objection.

~

The most practical definition
for self-forgiveness is
reasonable self-expectation.

Stand Up to Fear

You may think that you do not succeed because you lack competence, intelligence, charisma, or some other secret ingredient. But the lack of any of these characteristics is never as detrimental to success as fear can be.

Identify you fears, learn from your fears, but don't let your fears tell you what you can and cannot do.

~

Fear will stop you if you if you let it.
Don't let it.

Wise Fear

When fear is doing its *real* job, it will alert you to *real* dangers. Wise fear reminds you to wear your seat belt, to look both ways before you cross the road. Beware of the fear that tells you to avoid the road altogether.

~

Fear is sometimes wisdom,

and sometimes folly.

No Failure

Most of us spend too much time being afraid of failure when in fact there is not that much to fear --- for a couple of very good reasons:

1.) If you never give up, you never fail. The worst that can happen is you die trying.

2.) Learn from failure and it becomes success.

~

Hear with your ears,

rather than your fears.

Positive Anger

Anger is a powerful emotion and many people are afraid of it. You may be especially afraid of your own anger because you don't want to blame others for your problems. It is important that you pay attention to feelings of anger because they are telling you that something is not right. Anger itself is not a problem, as long as you learn to express it directly and respectfully.

~

Anger and blame

are not the same.

Redefining Strength

We need to stop equating strength of character with stubbornness. One of the most important lessons we can learn --- and pass on to our children --- is that knowing when, how and where to reach for help is strength, not weakness.

~

It takes more courage to reach out
for help than it does to
remain stubborn and isolated.

The Real Secret

One problem that everyone faces from time to time is impatience. Another is fatigue, commonly called "burn-out." To counter these common human maladies, practice what might be the only real secret to success: persistence.

~

Impatience is a waste of time.

Gratitude

Be careful to not use gratitude to beat yourself up --- as in "Since some people have it worse than me, I have no right to be dissatisfied or upset." Instead, remember that gratitude for the blessings in your life can co-exist with your dissatisfactions.

~

A feeling of gratitude is pleasant.

An expression of gratitude is useful.

Curiosity

Spend a day counting the number of times you hear yourself and others asking questions rhetorically. We are constantly asking perfectly good questions without the slightest interest in getting an answer.

Then spend a day demonstrating respect for others by asking questions with genuine curiosity.

~

Show respect: ask questions

with genuine curiosity.

Three Step Plan

When you decide to make a change, try this:

1.) Describe in detail where you are now --- the condition you want to change. (Point A)

2.) Describe in detail your desired destination --- the change you intend to make. (Point B)

3.) Then, and only then, begin to identify the obstacles you are likely to encounter as you travel from Point A to Point B.

Strangely, Step 2 of this plan is frequently neglected.

~

Don't waste your time "working on" your

negative messages.

Invest yourself in creating

their positive counterparts.

Looking In

When you are identifying obstacles between Points A and B, be sure to include a search for *internal obstacles*. Internal obstacles are the negative beliefs that are likely to set you up for self-sabotage.

~

Don't forget that you have the right to disagree with yourself.

A Time Saver

When you are taking an inventory of potential obstacles between you and your goal, categorize the obstacles as ...

1.) Certain to be encountered

2.) Possible to be encountered

3.) Not likely, but possible to be encountered.

It is interesting to note how much valuable time and energy we sometimes spend worrying about potential obstacles that we may never encounter.

~

Don't be blind to obstacles
in your path, but neither make
them your point of focus.

Worry-work

Most people who worry can identify one particular time of day when they tend to worry the most. Maybe it's first thing in the morning, or just before falling asleep at night. Maybe it's during the drive to work. Since it is not reasonable to expect yourself to just stop worrying, try this: Identify the time of day when you tend to worry the most, and really focus on worrying during that time. Do your best worrying, get the job done for the day, and then let it go --- until the next day.

Practice this focused worrying, using your very best work ethic. After a couple of weeks, try giving yourself a well deserved day off.

~

Schedule your worry, so that you are sure to have plenty of time. for more important things.

Focus

The next time you feel scattered, your mental energy shooting out in all directions, consider this: energy, like light, is more dynamically felt when it is concentrated in one direction, and most powerful when concentrated on one specific point. Focus your energy --- like light through a magnifying glass --- onto one specific point of your choosing.

Things will heat up.

~

If you <u>only</u> focus on the bottom-line, you will not rise to the top.

No Control

Beware of your tendency to react to feelings of fear and anger by trying to control something. More often than not, fear and anger show up when we are having trouble accepting that we are not in control. Tightening your grip is probably not the answer.

A good rule to follow is " when you are losing your grip, loosen your grip."

~

Negativity is an attempt to express fear that actually increases fear.

Experts

We are experts at dysfunctional communication. Think about how skilled you are at beginning a conversation and within a few seconds knowing that the conversation is a lost cause.

Here are some of the secrets to being a master of dysfunctional communication:

1.) Have only your agenda in mind.

2.) Interrupt often and don't listen unless you are doing the talking.

3.) Think fast, talk fast, generally be impulsive.

~

The best communication advice:

Slow Down!

Brain Rest

When your brain is tired, give it a rest by taking a few minutes to focus on just one thing at a time. Think of a person you like, or even just an object on your desk. Mentally repeat the name of the person or object, taking a deep breath with each repetition. Your brain really can rest when you do this.

No Excuse

If you have intended to take up meditation, but never seem to have enough time, try making your meditation one single breath: one full inhale and a complete exhale. Sit quietly, close your eyes, and take that one breath, allowing your mind to slow down, and your body to relax as you exhale.

From now on, you will have no excuse not to meditate. What are you going to say … that you don't have time for one breath?

~

One single breath can
transform your whole day.

The All Purpose Prayer

The next time you are in distress, and you are not sure what to pray for, try this one:

God,

Whatever the absolutely best prayer for this situation is, I am praying it now. Amen

~

*Have the good judgment
to let go of self-judgment.*

Taking Action

Thom Rutledge

Daily Decision

Every day you must decide to be either passive or proactive in your life. To be passive is to live by default, allowing the decisions of others to dictate the direction and the quality of your life. To be proactive is to live by decision, claiming full responsibility --- for better or worse --- for yourself.

~

Change is deniable, but inevitable.

Thought Power

You live as you think. Your feelings are determined more by your thoughts (interpretation of experience) than by the experiences themselves. Your actions are certainly determined by your thoughts --- by your beliefs about your environment, and about yourself.

The challenge is not to empower your thoughts, but to become aware of how powerful they already are. To be successful, you must learn to harness that power, and use it to your benefit, according to your choices.

~

Wanting something you don't have

can become a complaint or a goal.

It's your choice.

Deep Thoughts

Changing from the inside out takes more than repeating an affirmation 10 times every morning, and more than reading a few self-help books (including this one). To make the changes you desire, you must listen carefully to your daily self-talk, identifying very specifically what you are saying --- and what you are believing. Listen past the first or second levels of internal chatter, asking, "What am I really telling myself."

~

For the successful person, managing physical and mental energy is just as important as managing money. (Perhaps more important?)

Get Unstuck

Find the place inside you where you are repeatedly giving yourself the message that you need this person or that situation to be different in order for you to have what you want, or for you to feel the way you deserve to feel. If you are waiting for success to come to you from the outside in, you will die of old age waiting.

It starts and ends with you.

~

Self-esteem is more the product of your actions than of your feelings.

Don't Hold Your Breath

Make a list of all of those people and all of the situations that you tend to think need to change in order for you to have what you want. It's a good idea to make a list like this any time you are feeling stuck. If you want, extend this exercise by making notes about what specific changes you need from each person and each situation on your list.

When you have completed your list, burn it. Or you could try holding your breath until other people start to act right.

~

Each day, do your best
to make your life count,
without devaluing anyone else's.

Releasing Your Grip

When you insist on holding on to what is familiar, how can you possibly have a free hand to grasp something new? Letting go of the old, familiar ways can be frightening, but that doesn't mean that it can't be done.

Pay Day

Every morning when you wake up, it's pay day. You are given an allowance of mental energy for you to spend over the course of that day. It is entirely your choice how you will spend that allowance. Here are a couple of things to keep in mind:

1.) There will never be a shortage of people who will tell you how to spend your allowance, but it always remains your choice.

2.) Your allowance can be spent productively only in the present moment. Allowance spent feeling guilt or resentment about the past, or worrying about the future, is wasted.

Unicycle

Living in the present is like riding a unicycle. When you lean too far back (into the past), you fall. When you lean too far forward (into the future), you fall.

Living in the present is as difficult as learning to ride a unicycle: at first it will seem impossible, but it's not.

~

Transform the chaos of desperation into the focus of determination.

Identify the Split

The beliefs you express are only as good as their application. Take time to identify the discrepancy --- the split --- between the values you express and the values you demonstrate.

Without congruent action, your value system will do you about as much good as seeing a simple new invention on the market, and saying, "Oh, I thought of that years ago."

~

Close the gap between your expressed values and your behavioral values.

Two Questions

You cannot create lasting and positive change in your circumstances without changing yourself. No matter how much you know about what needs to change in the people and situations around you, the most powerful way – possibly the only way -- to make things happen is to ask yourself, "What am I doing here that is not working?" and "What do I need to do differently?"

~

If you don't see yourself as part of the problem, you won't be part of the solution.

Work from the Inside Out

To insure that you are pursuing a path of personal responsibility that will lead you to the success that you seek, keep this slogan in mind: *The first part of any conflict that I must resolve is that which is between me and me.*

A Starting Place

To look first at the conflict between self and self does not mean that you will not have legitimate problems with others --- your boss, your friend, your spouse or your colleague. And this is not meant to encourage the old self-victimization approach of habitually opting for self-blame. When you begin by resolving internal conflict, you are simply putting first things first. It's just the best place to start.

The Nature of Growth

When you begin problem resolution by looking within yourself, you are in essence going with the flow, complying with one of nature's laws: *growth moves from the inside out.* Growth, in the literal sense, is expansion. Expansion moves from the inside out.

~

*The change you seek
always begins with you.*

Who Can You Trust?

When you are serious about change, it is wise to take an inventory of all the times, and all the ways, you have been dishonest ... with yourself.

If you can't trust yourself, who can you trust?

Decide for Yourself

Here is a word to the wise: take in the information --- from this book and from any other source that seems potentially credible --- as raw material to be processed by your own good judgment. Accept nothing at face value. If an idea, a method, or a technique appears to have value for you, take it off the shelf, hold it in your hands, examine it, try it on, or try it out. Make adjustments according to your own good thinking. Accept it as your own only when you decide.

No One "Right Way"

Trust no one who will tell you that they have THE answer, THE way, THE plan, THE diet, THE anything. There are probably as many different approaches to genuine self-improvement as there are people, or at least as many different approaches as there are "self-helpers" (like me) on their soap boxes telling you how to do it.

Say No to All or Nothing

When making decisions about what works for you, use the line-item veto. You never have to accept anything all or nothing.

~

Respect others' opinions.

Trust your own good judgment.

Balance

Stand straight, with feet planted firmly, like a martial artist ready to meet an opposing force. This is your position when you are ready and willing to fight for yourself, ready to stand your grand, to not back down, to stand up for what you believe.

When you become distracted by the opposing force, allowing your anger to control you, you will become aggressive, and lose your balance.

~

Fight <u>against</u> someone,
and you will lose.
Fight <u>for</u> yourself,
and you will win.

Jump Start

One very effective way to stop yourself dead in your tracks is to take everything other people say and do personally. Is it personal? Sometimes it is, and sometimes it's not. The better question to ask is, "What can I learn from this person's response to me?"

~

When in doubt …

don't take it personally.

Learn the lesson and move on.

Homemade Motivation

If you want your car to go, you are going to need fuel. And if you plan on being successful, you are going to need motivation. Contrary to popular opinion, motivation doesn't just happen; you have to make your own.

Here are the ingredients you will need:

- Dissatisfaction

- Desire to make a change

- Belief that change is possible

- Willingness to do what it takes

Mix them all together and you will have a fine batch of motivation. In the event that you are not feeling motivated, check to see which ingredient is missing.

Push, Pull

You need both negative and positive motivation. *Negative motivation* is being motivated to avoid pain, discomfort or dissatisfaction. *Positive motivation* is the drive you feel pulling you toward pleasure. Think of it as being pushed and pulled at the same time.

~

Hope and fear are co-workers.

Fear pushes, and hope points the way.

From & To

With negative motivation, you decide who and what you are not or who you don't want to be. With positive motivation, you determine who and what you are and who you do want to be.

As you move *from* what is toxic in your life, you are free to move *to* what is healthy.

~

The question is not "Who am I?"

It is "Who will I choose to be?"

First Hand

A decision is a commitment, but you can always change your mind. As you approach a goal, you may find that what you thought the experience of attaining the goal would be is not the reality of the experience at all. You may not like it, but you could never have known this without first hand experience. So it makes good sense to be both committed *and* flexible --- occasionally re-evaluating your goals based on your constantly changing first hand experiences.

Death Bed Evaluation

Live your life in a way that will insure that when you are 112 and on your death bed, and someone asks you, "How do you think you did?", you will be able to answer, "Pretty good I think."

Live today, and everyday, in that same way --- just in case you get run over by a bus tomorrow.

~

Live according to

The Regret-Reduction Program

Act Now

Imagine a football team that becomes so involved in planning their strategy for the big game that they forget to leave the locker room to go on the playing field, or the student who never applies the knowledge acquired from years of study.

Self-help books and seminars are classroom time, locker-room preparations. The real deal is out there, in your day-to-day, unpredictable life.

Don't forget to put yourself into the game.

~

Success is built,

not created in an instant.

Off the Top

Taking care to live a life you will be proud of is like saving money: you cannot wait until the last minute, or even tomorrow, since tomorrow may be the last minute. You have to start now. Like saving money, you have to "take it off the top." If you wait for "extra money" to save, there will be no savings. If you wait for "extra time" or "extra energy" to live the life you want to live, you may never get around to it.

~

Be a person you would
be proud to know.

Knowing Yourself

Simple Truth

It seems that the most important truths are very simple. But these are the truths that we forget time and again. The good news is that we have each other to remind us of this simple truth: that we are all perfectly imperfect human beings, planted here on planet earth to do the best we can --- nothing more and nothing less.

~

It's good to spend time wondering who you are, without settling on any one particular answer.

Being Vulnerable

Vulnerability is not the same as weakness. Of course, you need to use your good judgment about how much to share --- and with whom --- but do take the risk of letting others get to know who you really are. When you do this, you will understand that being vulnerable takes considerable strength and courage.

~

Success involves taking one risk after another, with little breaks in between.

Formula

Here is a simple formula for self-responsibility:

Learning from the past

+

Planning for the future

+

Living in the present

Pop Test

It is a mistake to assume that you have good intentions. Intention is like a muscle: if you neglect it, it will atrophy. Every morning after you brush your teeth and do a few push ups, give yourself this little pop test: *What is my intention for this day?*

~

Intention is a daily responsibility.

Being & Doing

There are two general sources from which you gain and maintain self-esteem: "being" and "doing." The more familiar source is "doing." You know how to feel good or bad about yourself depending on how you choose to act in your daily life. The more elusive source of self-esteem is "being." This is the self-esteem that is unconditional, the inner-knowing that you are a good and worthy person, not better or worse than anyone else.

You need self-esteem from both sources. Think of them as the two food groups of self-esteem.

Your Opinion

It is important to care about what other people think about you, but it is even more important that you not allow other people's opinions to define you.

~

Whose opinion do you predominantly use to evaluate yourself?

And what is your opinion?

Recharge

If you are usually around a lot of people, be sure to find some time for yourself on a regular basis. Time alone can be time to recharge your battery, time to reflect, and time to just plain rest.

Be careful to not use time alone to beat yourself up.

~

Solitude is vital.

Isolation can be deadly.

Giving & Receiving

You have been told that giving is better than receiving, but you may not have been told that both giving and receiving are necessary to insure your wellbeing. Sometimes the missing piece --- and the harder work --- is learning to receive.

Teaching

If you don't know how to play the guitar, then you will not be very good at giving guitar lessons. This is common sense --- common sense that is sometimes not applied to other aspects of our lives. If you want to teach someone to be self-caring it really is best for you to practice what you are teaching.

~

"Do as I say, not as I do"
is not a very good lesson plan.

Lessons

If you wanted to play the guitar, but did not know how, what could you do? Take lessons, of course. If you want to take good care of yourself, but you don't know how, what could you do?

~

When you don't know how

to do something,

taking lessons is more

productive than self-criticism.

Belief

What do you believe? And do you put your beliefs into practice in your daily life? In other words, how much of what you believe do you really believe?

~

For your actions to be congruent

with your beliefs is to

earn your own respect.

Magnet Questions

Being "right" is over-rated. Rather than concerning yourself with being right, focus on all that you can learn as you move through your life. A good question, asked of yourself or of others, will act as a powerful magnet, literally attracting information and knowledge. Collect all the information and knowledge each question can draw to it. Don't settle for just one answer, no matter how "right" it may seem.

~

Forget about finding

the right answers.

Just make a list

of very good questions.

Intelligence

Intelligence is like any other tool. It can be used constructively or destructively. Make a point to check in with yourself on a regular basis to see how you are doing with your intelligence.

~

Can you tell when you are using your intelligence to avoid learning?

Not Stupid

Ignorance is not stupidity; it is simply the state of not knowing. Not acknowledging your ignorance, on the other hand, can be very stupid.

~

Wisdom is the

accumulated knowledge

of our ignorance

Knowing When to Quit

You know the expression, "quit while you are ahead." Often this is good advice. Then there are other times when you will be wise to "quit while you are behind." Knowing when to quit is important, but not always easy.

~

We all need limits. Occasionally it is important to "No" thyself.

Absent Minded

Have you ever walked from one room to the next, only to forget why you came into that room? To resolve the mystery, you trace your steps back until you remember.

In the same way, by the time you make it from childhood to adulthood, you may have forgotten your early dreams and intentions. Trace your steps back until you remember what you wanted --- and intended --- to do with your life.

~

Your purpose can remain clear,

even when your path is not.

Courage

Courage is a natural part of us all. The successful person's task is not to create courage, but to find it within herself, and to cultivate it as part of daily life. Courage in the humdrum of daily life is the extra nudge, or surge of confidence, that we all need in order to step toward the lessons and challenges that scare us.

~

Courage is a daily practice.

Power

Genuine power has nothing to do with controlling other people or getting what you need through manipulation. Genuine power is the power to make your own choices, without hiding behind a shield of victimization (*I had no choice, I had to do it.*)

Genuine power is the power --- and the courage --- to step forward and claim full responsibility for yourself, mistakes and all.

~

Who you are is a matter of
choice --- or more accurately,
a matter of many choices.

Humility

Humility is a wonderful asset to the successful man or woman. Humility is not about being in a "one down" position; it is about being on a level playing field. The truly humble person recognizes his place among all other imperfect human beings, neither better nor worse than anyone else.

~

Humility is an essential ingredient to genuine success.

Being Wrong

Don't apologize just to keep the peace, but when you are wrong, admit it. The strength of your character will benefit more from a willingness to acknowledge error than it will from a track record of "being right."

~

When you're right, you're right.

When you're wrong, admit it!

Uncertainty

We long for certainty in a world whose nature is uncertainty. The ultimate challenge is to live with acceptance of all that we don't know, and all that we don't control.

~

We hate uncertainty, we hate change, and the only thing certain about life is change.

Big Difference

There is a big difference between recognizing your mistakes and shortcomings to support the big I-Told-You-So-Within (*I told you that you couldn't do it. You should not have even tried.*), and confronting the same mistakes and shortcomings to improve yourself.

~

Don't waste your regrets.

Learn the lessons.

Self-Respect

Self-respect is the most important respect that you can earn. To earn your own respect you must live responsibly, you must identify and clarify your personal value system, and act on a daily basis in accordance with that value system. In other words, you will respect yourself to the degree that you do not violate your own value system.

~

The best measure of self-esteem

is the degree of comfort

you have in your own company.

Good Question

Ask yourself, "How can I live this day in a way that even if I were later given the opportunity to change it, I wouldn't want to?"

~

Responsible thoughts are only useful when they lead to responsible action.

Not the Real Deal

Grandiosity and arrogance should not be mistaken for positive self-esteem any more than feelings of worthlessness and shame should be mistaken for true humility.

~

Often, attempts to take responsibility for others is a clever way to avoid responsibilities of our own.

Why?

It is very easy to ask why. *Why has this happened? Why him and not me? Why do I keep running into the same problem over and over again? Why can't I ever catch a break?*

Many experts will tell you to avoid the why-question altogether, saying that it will only keep you stuck. What will really keep you stuck is asking why, and then ignoring the answer.

Usually the answer to the why-question involves accepting the reality of the situation --- *including that life just ain't fair* --- and challenging yourself to change your approach.

~

When you ask why, listen
for an answer, then do
something with that answer.

Some Clean Advice

Approach your life like you might approach the daily practice of washing dishes. When the dishes are washed, you feel good, but if you expect that the dishes will stay washed, you are setting yourself up for disappointment.

As soon as the last coffee cup is washed and placed in the dish drainer, we all know what happens … another dirty dish.

The Measure of Life

- Know what you believe.
- Allow your beliefs to grow and change.
- Put your beliefs into practice --- daily practice.
- Never give up.

Follow these simple principles, and with or without the trappings of material success, you will be truly successful.

~

If life is an essay test, what question are you working on now?

Resting

Life is a long race. You will have the need to stop to catch your breath now and then. Sometimes you will sprint when you would do better to pace yourself.

Rest ... but never quit.

Traffic

Stress management gurus will often claim to help people "reduce their stress." This is a little bit like a driving instructor promising to reduce the amount of traffic so that your driving experience will be easier. It can be accomplished in a learning environment, but not in real life.

Think of stress as the traffic in your life. Sure, avoid predictable rush hour traffic jams whenever you can. But more importantly, learn to be patient and become a good driver.

The Key

Repetition is the key to mastery.

Repetition is the key to mastery.

Repetition is the key to mastery.

Repetition is the key to mastery.

Repetition is the key to mastery.

Repetition is the key to mastery.

Repetition is the key to mastery.

Repetition is the key to mastery.

Repetition is the key to mastery.

Repetition is the key to mastery.

Repetition is the key to mastery.

~

Read this book again.

About the Author

Thom Rutledge is the author of several books, including *Embracing Fear, The Self-Forgiveness Handbook, Earning Your Own Respect, Nutshell Essays* and *Simple Truth*. He has been featured on NBC's Today Show, Anderson Cooper 360, Fox News, Australia's Channel 10 and had consulted with The Dr. Phil Show.

To stay current with what Thom is up to, join him on Facebook: www.facebook.com/thom.rutledge.9

Or visit www.thomrutledge.com

If you have enjoyed and/or benefited from *The Greater Possibilities,* please visit Thom's website to learn more about his other books, his workshops and other available services, including Skype/Telephone consultations. Also visit Thom's FREE Download Page for short articles and handouts that you might find helpful personally and/or that you might use for therapy and support groups.

Included at the bottom of the FREE Download page there are two free book excerpts: Chapter One of *Embracing Fear* and the Introduction and first 2 chapters of *The Self-Forgiveness Handbook.*